Rest in
GOD
a prayer journal

WITH 100 PRAYERS
AND SCRIPTURES
FOR DAILY...

Yvon

Rest in GOD

a prayer journal

WITH 100 PRAYERS AND SCRIPTURES FOR DAILY NEEDS

Rest in GOD

a prayer journal

WITH 100 PRAYERS
AND SCRIPTURES
FOR DAILY NEEDS

By
Yvonne M. Morgan

Foreword written by Carla Pollard
Founder of Created to Climb Ministry

Arabelle Publishing, LLC
Chesterfield, VA

TO BILL, MY WONDERFUL HUSBAND

What a ride we've had so far, I pray it lasts for years to come. Thank you for all your incredible support. I love you.

A Heart for God and Others

My connection with the author of this book, Yvonne M. Morgan, is simple: we share a common love for God and others. We both express this love through intimate times of prayer and meditation on the Scriptures, and through sharing with others the importance of developing a devotional life. Yvonne's testimony is understood through the prayers she shares from her heart and through the biblical promises quoted within the pages of this devotional journal. Yvonne has learned the art of resting in God through difficult times. She believes God answers prayers; her desire for you is to believe him too. Yvonne has witnessed God turn her mountains into molehills.

Both Yvonne and I believe something powerful takes place when we quote God's word and share our hearts with him. We see mountains removed, blinded eyes opened, desires fulfilled, and lives restored. Through our prayers, we bring the intentions of Heaven to Earth. This book contains both God's promises and simple prayers uttered from a faith-filled heart.

I want you to think of this devotional as a new adventure with God. When we begin any new adventure, it is always a good thing to look to someone with experience. Within the Gospels we see Jesus spending private time in prayer. He was such a prayerful leader his disciples asked him to teach them how to pray. From his example we learn the importance of going to a quiet place to pray and read the Bible. It is through those times God blesses us with his presence and meets our needs. Whether you are a beginner in your devotional life, or a mature believer who prays continually, this book will help guide you in developing a closer relationship with Jesus.

Yvonne has spent many hours reflecting on God's word and penning down authentic prayers to guide you in your journey of faith. She has thoughtfully provided space within this prayer devotional for you to capture the words of your heart, other promises from God, and the answers to your unique prayers. As you take advantage of this special feature, Rest in God: A Prayer Journal with 100 Prayers & Scriptures for Daily Needs will prove to be a treasured keepsake and testimony of your faith for generations to come.

It is my prayer for you, Dear Reader, that you take hold of the promises and commit your heart to spend quality time with Jesus as you lift these prayers to Heaven and reflect on the Scriptures. May the God of Heaven comfort your hearts and show himself strong on your behalf.

Carla G. Pollard
Christian minister and author
www.carlagpollard.com

PRAYERS OFFER US
a direct connection with the Creator of the Universe.

Prayers provide us personal access to the throne room of God so we can talk with our Heavenly Father about our fears, our joys, our problems, and our praise. But, sometimes, we struggle to find the right words that speak from our hearts. In this book, it is my hope you find the words to better express your feelings to God in prayer. Expand on the prayers in this book to develop your own personal prayers. Scripture references are included to encourage you in your prayer life.

prayers FOR COMFORT

When stress and fear threaten to overtake us, we can turn to God for comfort. Throughout the Bible, we see how God's people sought him for strength and courage in troubling times. This section offers prayers and scripture references for when you need God's comforting touch in your life.

Dear Lord,

Thank you that I can approach your mercy seat and seek you. I know that you will answer me and deliver me from my fears. I desire to receive strength in this time of great difficulty. Father, you are my rock in whom I gain strength.

Amen

Hebrews 4:16

Let us then approach God's throne of grace with confidence, so that we may receive mercy and find grace to help us in our time of need.

MY
Prayers

_____

_____

_____

_____

_____

_____

_____

_____

ANSWERED
Prayers

_____

_____

_____

_____

_____

_____

_____

_____

Dear Loving Savior,

Thank you for allowing us to bring our fears to you in prayer. Help us to guard our hearts when we hear of tragic news in your world. Remind us to turn to you in prayer when our world feels out of control. In Jesus' Name.

Amen

Joshua 1:9

"Have I not commanded you? Be strong and courageous. Do not be afraid; do not be discouraged, for the LORD your God will be with you wherever you go."

MY
Prayers

ANSWERED
Prayers

Dearest Jesus,

Thank you for showing me the beauty of my hard places today. Help me feel your presence when my back is against a wall of troubles. Help me remember to pray for your will to be done and not mine.

Amen

2 Corinthians 1:3-4

Praise be to the God and Father of our Lord Jesus Christ, the Father of compassion and the God of all comfort, who comforts us in all our troubles, so that we can comfort those in any trouble with the comfort we ourselves receive from God.

MY
Prayers

ANSWERED
Prayers

Father,

Thank you for wiping away every tear and comforting us in every circumstance. Thank you for reminding us the Jesus understands us and our emotions. Please help me to turn to you for when my feelings are raw and out of control. In Jesus' Name.

Amen

Matthew 11:28-30

"Come to me, all you who are weary and burdened, and I will give you rest. Take my yoke upon you and learn from me, for I am gentle and humble in heart, and you will find rest for your souls. For my yoke is easy and my burden is light."

MY
Prayers

ANSWERED
Prayers

God of Peace,

Thank you for holding us firmly when we are broken-hearted. Thank you for standing by our side and allowing us to feel your physical presence when we are grieving. Please help us to remember in prayer, those who are crushed in Spirit and need help to face the future. In Jesus' Name.

Amen

Psalm 23:4

"Even though I walk through the darkest valley, I will fear no evil, for you are with me; your rod and your staff, they comfort me.

MY
Prayers

ANSWERED
Prayers

Heavenly Father,

As the days of winter and darkness drag on,
please help me to know you are still with me.
Help me to look forward to the new life found
for in spring. Prepare my heart for renewal. In
Jesus' Name.

Amen

Deuteronomy 31:8

The Lord himself goes before you and will be
with you; he will never leave you nor forsake
you. Do not be afraid; do not be discouraged.

MY
Prayers

ANSWERED
Prayers

Father,

I am comforted by your Word. My soul finds rest in God. My salvation comes only from you. You are my rock and salvation. Nothing shakes me because of you. I will dwell in the secret place of the Most High God, and in you I trust. I glorify you for protecting me from the evil one.

Amen

Psalm 27:12

The LORD is my light and my salvation— whom shall I fear? The LORD is the stronghold of my life— of whom shall I be afraid?

MY
Prayers

_____

_____

_____

_____

_____

_____

_____

ANSWERED
Prayers

_____

_____

_____

_____

_____

_____

_____

Lord Jesus Christ,

Son of God. Have mercy on me, a sinner.

Amen

2 Corinthians 1:1-4

Paul, an apostle of Christ Jesus by the will of God, and Timothy our brother, To the church of God in Corinth, together with all his holy people throughout Achaia: Grace and peace to you from God our Father and the Lord Jesus Christ. Praise be to the God and Father of our Lord Jesus Christ, the Father of compassion and the God of all comfort, who comforts us in all our troubles, so that we can comfort those in any trouble with the comfort we ourselves receive from God.

MY
Prayers

_____

_____

_____

_____

_____

_____

_____

ANSWERED
Prayers

_____

_____

_____

_____

_____

_____

_____

Lord,

I need you. Come to my rescue. Hear my prayer.

Amen

Isaiah 40:1-5

"Comfort, comfort my people, says your God. Speak tenderly to Jerusalem and proclaim to her that her hard service has been completed, that her sin has been paid for, that she has received from the LORD's hand double for all her sins. A voice of one calling: "In the wilderness prepare the way for the LORD; make straight in the desert a highway for our God. Every valley shall be raised up, every mountain and hill made low; the rough ground shall become level, the rugged places a plain. And the glory of the LORD will be revealed, and all people will see it together. For the mouth of the LORD has spoken."

MY
Prayers

ANSWERED
Prayers

Lord,

I reach out to you for your guidance. Please show me which way to turn. Calm my anxious thoughts, speak into my mind. Strengthen me when I feel weary. Bring clarity into my visions and dreams. I trust that you are with me, no matter where I go.

Amen

Psalm 32:8

I will instruct you and teach you in the way you should go; I will counsel you with my loving eye on you.

MY
Prayers

ANSWERED
Prayers

Lord,

You give power to the weak, and you strengthen the powerless. I recognize my failures, and I know that only your strength can carry me through this turmoil. Help me to remain positive, and I speak only in your strength even in my weakness. I declare this prayer in your name.

Amen

Psalm 119:76

May your unfailing love be my comfort, according to your promise to your servant.

MY
Prayers

ANSWERED
Prayers

My Loving Father,

Thank you for watching over all of our steps. Thank you for directing our steps to keep me safe and secure. Please help us to remember that when things don't go as planned, that you are in control, and your plans are the best. In Jesus' name.

Amen

Psalm 9:9

The LORD is a refuge for the oppressed, a stronghold in times of trouble.

MY
Prayers

_____

_____

_____

_____

_____

_____

_____

ANSWERED
Prayers

_____

_____

_____

_____

_____

_____

My Strength and Shield,

Thank you for rewarding our faithfulness, especially during trying times. Thank you for standing by our side and giving us the words and strength when trials set in. Please help us to remember in prayer those who face persecution for their faith. In Jesus' Name.

Amen

Psalm 18:2

The Lord is my rock, my fortress and my deliverer; my God is my rock, in whom I take refuge, my shield and the horn of my salvation, my stronghold.

MY
Prayers

ANSWERED
Prayers

prayers FOR GUIDANCE

We all stray from the path God prepared for us. Often, we feel unsure of which way to go in life. God's guidance is a simple prayer away. He wants to help us walk in his way. This section provides prayers and scriptures to help find the guidance we seek.

Abba Father,

Thank you for waiting for me and for giving me eternal life. Help me to spread your good news so others may join us in Heaven. I wait for your glorious return when your time is right. In Jesus' Name.

Amen

Philippians 4:6-7

" Do not be anxious about anything, but in everything by prayer and supplication with thanksgiving let your requests be made known to God. And the peace of God, which surpasses all understanding, will guard your hearts and your minds in Christ Jesus. "

MY
Prayers

ANSWERED
Prayers

Almighty God,
Your blessed Son was led by the Spirit to be
tempted by Satan: Come quickly to help us who
are assaulted by many temptations; and, as you
know our weaknesses, let each one find you
mighty to save; through Jesus Christ your Son
our Lord,

Amen

James 1:5

" If any of you lacks wisdom, you should ask God,
who gives generously to all without finding fault,
and it will be given to you. "

MY
Prayers

ANSWERED
Prayers

Come, Lord Jesus,

Show me Your ways. Direct me on the way to go.
Guide my feet as I tread this path called life. Bless
me and keep me today and every day.

Amen

Proverbs 3:5-6

" Trust in the Lord with all your heart and lean
not on your own understanding; in all your ways
submit to him, and he will make your paths
straight. "

MY
Prayers

ANSWERED
Prayers

Dear Heavenly Father,

Thank you for allowing us to participate in your mission on earth. Help me to remain faithful even when the roadway leads me through the valley. Help me to persevere and reap your reward for my faithfulness. In Jesus' Name. *Amen*

Psalm 37:4

" Take delight in the Lord, and he will give you the desires of your heart. "

MY
Prayers

ANSWERED
Prayers

Dear Jesus,

I pray my steps today took me where you wanted me to go. Direct my path again tomorrow, and every day you grant me. I continually look for your guidance. I love you, my Lord.

Amen

Isaiah 30:21

" Whether you turn to the right or to the left, your ears will hear a voice behind you, saying, "This is the way; walk in it. "

MY
Prayers

ANSWERED
Prayers

Dearest Jesus,

I confess that you are the one true way to eternal life. Please give me your words to share with others to show them the truth of who you are. Protect me from those who teach something different. In Jesus' Name.

Amen

John 16:33

" I have told you these things, so that in me you may have peace. In this world you will have trouble. But take heart! I have overcome the world. "

MY
Prayers

ANSWERED
Prayers

Dear Heavenly Father,

Thank you for holding me accountable in my faith. Thank you for loving us enough to want to teach us your ways. Please help us to remember and accept the disciple you give to us. In Jesus' Name.

Amen

Psalm 37:4

" Take delight in the Lord, and he will give you the desires of your heart. "

MY
Prayers

ANSWERED
Prayers

Dearest Jesus,

Thank you for loving us unconditionally and accepting us even with our imperfections. Thank you for reminding us that Jesus knows us even better than we know ourselves and still loves us. Please help me to drop my mask and live only for you. In Jesus' Name.

Amen

Romans 8:28

And we know that in all things God works for the good of those who love him, who have been called according to his purpose.

MY
Prayers

ANSWERED
Prayers

Father God,

Thank you for loving us so deeply. When we try to complicate our faith, show us how to keep it simple. Remind us to believe and accept Jesus into our hearts. Help us to remember to share the good news of the gift of salvation with others. In Jesus' Name.

Amen

Proverbs 12:15

" The way of fools seems right to them, but the wise listen to advice. "

MY
Prayers

ANSWERED
Prayers

Father,

Clear my sleepy head and fill my mind with expectation. Awake and energize my heart with love in action. Ignite my Spirit and set this day on fire with promise. Make the ordinary extraordinary. Help me to see every waking moment is full of hope because of you.

Amen

Proverbs 16:9

" In their hearts humans plan their course, but the Lord establishes their steps. "

MY
Prayers

_____

_____

_____

_____

_____

_____

ANSWERED
Prayers

_____

_____

_____

_____

_____

_____

God,

Please enlighten my mind with truth, inflame my heart with love, inspire my will with courage, enrich my life with service. Pardon what I have been, sanctify what I am, and order what I shall be.

Amen

2 Peter 1:3

" His divine power has given us everything we need for a godly life through our knowledge of him who called us by his own glory and goodness. "

MY
Prayers

ANSWERED
Prayers

Heavenly Father,

Forgive me for the times I stubbornly demand my way. Teach to submit to Your will no matter what happens. I want to pray like Jesus in the face of an uncertain future. Thank you, Jesus, for loving me always.

Amen

Colossians 3:17

> And whatever you do, whether in word or deed, do it all in the name of the Lord Jesus, giving thanks to God the Father through him.

MY
Prayers

ANSWERED
Prayers

Heavenly Father,

Please be with me as I labor today. Help me re-member to do everything in love and to work hard as if laboring for you. Thank you for every-thing.

Amen

1 Peter 5:7

" Cast all your anxiety on him because he cares for you. "

MY
Prayers

ANSWERED
Prayers

Father God,

I pray for all that I do and say will be a witness to Jesus. I pray I will regularly spend time abiding in Jesus and that the work I do will bring glory to Christ and not to myself.

Amen

Philippians 2:13

" for it is God who works in you to will and to act in order to fulfill his good purpose. "

MY
Prayers

ANSWERED
Prayers

Jesus,

You are the potter, and I am the clay. Please mold my life to fit your plans. Give me a heart that runs after you daily. Allow my eyes to see the world as you see it. Help me reach out in love to those you show me. In Jesus' Name.

Amen

I Corinthians 10:13

" So whether you eat or drink or whatever you do, do it all for the glory of God. "

MY
Prayers

_____

_____

_____

_____

_____

_____

_____

_____

ANSWERED
Prayers

_____

_____

_____

_____

_____

_____

_____

Lord Jesus,

Please forgive me for all the times I try to hide behind a multitude of words. Please help me to remember that you already know everything about me. Teach me to make my words count. Thank you, Jesus.

Amen

Proverbs 11:14

" For lack of guidance a nation falls, but victory is won through many advisers. "

MY
Prayers

_____

_____

_____

_____

_____

_____

_____

ANSWERED
Prayers

_____

_____

_____

_____

_____

_____

_____

My God,

Give me a thirst for your word. I want to read
and understand the love letter you wrote to us in
the Bible. Teach me and lead me to your truths.
Thank you.

Amen

James 1:5-6

"If any of you lacks wisdom, you should ask
God, who gives generously to all without finding fault, and it will be given to you. But when
you ask, you must believe and not doubt, because the one who doubts is like a wave of the
sea, blown and tossed by the wind"

MY
Prayers

ANSWERED
Prayers

My Heavenly Father,

Thank you for loving me enough to want to spend eternity with me. I am awed by the thought of worshipping you as part of the great multitude. Please forgive me for the times when I take Heaven for granted. Please give me the desire to share my faith with others so they can join us. In Jesus' Name.

Amen

John 3:16

" For God so loved the world that he gave his one and only Son, that whoever believes in him shall not perish but have eternal life. "

MY
Prayers

ANSWERED
Prayers

Father,

Our lives are but a breath, and our time is in your hands. Turmoil fills the days of our lives as we watch the ways of the world. It helps us to keep our eyes on you alone for everything we need. Provide for our daily needs and forgive us for our trespasses. We ask this in your Holy Name.

Amen

Hebrews 13:5

Keep your lives free from the love of money and be content with what you have, because God has said, "Never will I leave you; never will I forsake you."

MY
Prayers

ANSWERED
Prayers

Father,

Speak to me, Lord, for your servant is listening.

Amen

Proverbs 15:22

66 Plans fail for lack of counsel, but with
many advisers they succeed. 99

MY
Prayers

ANSWERED
Prayers

prayers

TO HELP US LIVE IN HARMONY
WITH ONE ANOTHER

When God created Adam, he did not want Adam to be alone, so he created Eve. God created us to live in community and in harmony with one another. But sometimes our relationships become difficult as we find a discourse develops. This section contains prayers and scriptures to help us maintain those relationships in a Godly manner.

Abba Father,

Thank you for showing us our neighbors through the story of the Good Samaritan. Thank you for reminding us to love all of our neighbors, even those who are different from us. Please help me to love all those you place in my path. In Jesus' Name.

Amen

1 Corinthians 10:11

"I appeal to you, brothers and sisters, in the name of our Lord Jesus Christ, that all of you agree with one another in what you say and that there be no divisions among you, but that you be perfectly united in mind and thought."

MY
Prayers

ANSWERED
Prayers

Dear Father in Heaven,

I argue and disagree with those I love from time to time. Please help me to remember to end the hard conversation with a blessing so we can part in peace. Thank you for teaching me your ways and for helping me to live in harmony with all my brothers and sisters. In Jesus' Name.

Amen

Ephesians 4:11-14

So Christ himself gave the apostles, the prophets, the evangelists, the pastors and teachers, to equip his people for works of service, so that the body of Christ may be built up until we all reach unity in the faith and in the knowledge of the Son of God and become mature, attaining to the whole measure of the fullness of Christ.

MY
Prayers

ANSWERED
Prayers

Dear God,

Thank you for the gift of family and friends. Holding them in my heart is one of the most precious things I can ever do. Bless everyone, for they deserve all the goodness You have given to me. If I do something wrong today, please forgive me.

Amen

Colossians 3:13-14

"Bear with each other and forgive one another if any of you has a grievance against someone. Forgive as the Lord forgave you. And over all these virtues put on love, which binds them all together in perfect unity."

MY
Prayers

ANSWERED
Prayers

Dear Heavenly Father,

Thank you for breathing life into me. Help me to use your breath in worship and praise back to you. Show me when I wrongly use my words when I speak to others. In Jesus' Name.

Amen

John 17:23

I in them and you in me—so that they may be brought to complete unity. Then the world will know that you sent me and have loved them even as you have loved me.

MY
Prayers

_____

_____

_____

_____

_____

_____

_____

_____

ANSWERED
Prayers

_____

_____

_____

_____

_____

_____

_____

_____

Dear Heavenly Father,

You taught us the importance of family heritage. Today, we pray for the health and protection of each member of our family. Thank you for the teachings of our ancestors. Bless us and keep us all the days of our lives.

Amen

Psalm 133:1

"How good and pleasant it is when God's people live together in unity!"

MY
Prayers

ANSWERED
Prayers

Dear Jesus,

Let me always be mindful of how I use my freedoms. Teach me to be aware of how my ways affect those around me. Thank you for allowing us freedom in our daily lives and for always loving us. In the precious Name of Jesus.

Amen

1 Peter 3:8

"Finally, all of you, be like-minded, be sympathetic, love one another, be compassionate and humble."

MY
Prayers

ANSWERED
Prayers

Holy One in Heaven,

Thank you for loving us despite all our faults. Thank you for teaching us to watch our words, so they reflect your love always. Please help us to remember to think about our words before we offer them to those around us. In Jesus' Name.

Amen

1 John 4:12

No one has ever seen God; but if we love one another, God lives in us and his love is made complete in us.

MY
Prayers

ANSWERED
Prayers

Lord,

Thank you for the gift of parents or the gift of those who raised us. Thank you for reminding us to honor them and love them. Please help me to find the time to visit and call them often. In Jesus' Name.

Amen

Ephesians 4:3

"Make every effort to keep the unity of the Spirit through the bond of peace."

MY
Prayers

_____

_____

_____

_____

_____

_____

_____

_____

ANSWERED
Prayers

_____

_____

_____

_____

_____

_____

_____

_____

My God,

Thank you for the eternal love you give us every day. Thank you for reminding me to love my neighbor as myself. Please direct me to those that need to feel that love today. In Jesus' Name.

Amen

Romans 12:16

"Live in harmony with one another. Do not be proud but be willing to associate with people of low position. Do not be conceited."

MY
Prayers

ANSWERED
Prayers

My Lord and my God,

Thank you for showing us how to help others in the world. Please open our eyes to see those less fortunate than us and provide ways to support those in need. Remind us to pray daily for those forgotten by the world. In Jesus' Name.

Amen

Romans 6:5

" For if we have been united with him in a death like his, we will certainly also be united with him in a resurrection like his. "

MY
Prayers

ANSWERED
Prayers

prayers *OF PRAISE*

Often, many of us spend our prayer time in petitioning the Lord for our wants and needs. God already knows our needs and answers before we ask. We must always remember to offer our praises and thanksgiving for all the Lord does for us daily. This section includes prayers and verses to remind us to be thankful for our many blessings.

Dear Heavenly Father,

Thank you for providing us with the wisdom in the Bible. Thank you for teaching us to follow the path that leads to you. Help us always to remember to trust in you and not in on our own ways and resources. In Jesus, Name.

Amen

1 Chronicles 16:23-25

"Sing to the LORD, all the earth; proclaim his salvation day after day. Declare his glory among the nations, his marvelous deeds among all peoples. For great is the LORD and most worthy of praise; he is to be feared above all gods."

MY
Prayers

ANSWERED
Prayers

Dear Jesus,

Thank you for blessing us with the gift of your Son, our Savior. Thank you for teaching us about the blessings we receive from giving to others. Help us always to be gracious givers in a world of consumers. In Jesus' Name.

Amen

Daniel 2:20

"and said: "Praise be to the name of God for ever and ever; wisdom and power are his.

MY
Prayers

_____

_____

_____

_____

_____

_____

_____

_____

ANSWERED
Prayers

_____

_____

_____

_____

_____

_____

_____

_____

Dear Jesus,

I want to offer you my sincerest thanks for every-thing your hands provide me. Sometimes, I for-get that all I have is from you. Thank you for my family and my friends. I praise your Holy Name for all my undeserved blessings. Praise Your Name forever and ever.

Amen

Deuteronomy 10:21

" He is the one you praise; he is your God, who performed for you those great and awesome wonders you saw with your own eyes. "

MY
Prayers

ANSWERED
Prayers

Dear Lord,

Thank you for revealing all your promises to us. Thank you for being faithful in what you have promised and that we can rest in your truths. Teach us to reflect on the promises when we feel lost and lonely in the world. In Jesus' Name.

Amen

Jeremiah 20:13

"Sing to the LORD! Give praise to the LORD! He rescues the life of the needy from the hands of the wicked."

MY
Prayers

ANSWERED
Prayers

Dearest Father in Heaven,

Thank you for your unmerited gift of grace in our lives. When we feel lost in our sins, please forgive us with your perfect grace. Remind us to ask for your forgiveness daily. In Jesus' Name.

Amen

Psalm 75:1

We praise you, God, we praise you, for your Name is near; people tell of your wonderful deeds.

MY
Prayers

ANSWERED
Prayers

Father God,

Thank you for loving us no matter the situations we find ourselves. Thank you for your faithfulness in loving us every day. Show us to look to you and your love when we feel scared by worldly events. In Jesus' Name.

Amen

John 4:24

"
God is spirit, and his worshipers must worship in the Spirit and in truth.
"

MY
Prayers

_____

_____

_____

_____

_____

_____

_____

ANSWERED
Prayers

_____

_____

_____

_____

_____

_____

_____

I come before you, oh, Lord.

As the sun rises, may your hope rise in me. As the birds sing, may your love flow out of me. As the light floods into this new day, may your joy shine through me. I come before you so I may carry your hope, love, and joy today in my heart

Amen

Psalm 99:9

" Exalt the LORD our God and worship at his holy mountain, for the LORD our God is holy. "

MY
Prayers

_____

_____

_____

_____

_____

_____

ANSWERED
Prayers

_____

_____

_____

_____

_____

_____

_____

Lord Jesus,

As we contemplate your humble birth, we see the shadows of the cross on the horizon. Let us remember that we are an Easter people. Thank you for the gift of the resurrection and the chance for eternal life.

Amen

Hebrews 12:28-29

"Therefore, since we are receiving a kingdom that cannot be shaken, let us be thankful, and so worship God acceptably with reverence and awe, for our "God is a consuming fire."

MY
Prayers

ANSWERED
Prayers

My Father,

Thank you for the beauty of a spring morning. Thank you for reminding me to be still occasion- ally. Please let me hear your whispers in the still- ness of my day. Let your presence overwhelm my weary soul. In Jesus' Name.

Amen

Psalm 86:9-10

"

All the nations you have made will come and worship before you, Lord; they will bring glory to your name. For you are great and do marvel- ous deeds; you alone are God.

"

MY
Prayers

ANSWERED
Prayers

My Lord and my Savior,

I praise your holy Name this morning. Your goodness and grace leave me breathless as I try to comprehend all your hand provides. Thank you, dearest Lord.

Amen

2 Kings 17:38-39

> Do not forget the covenant I have made with you, and do not worship other gods. Rather, worship the LORD your God; it is he who will deliver you from the hand of all your enemies.

MY
Prayers

ANSWERED
Prayers

My Lord and Savior,

Thank you for using such simple things as salt to teach us about sharing the gospel. Thank you for allowing us to share our saltiness with those who need you. Help us always to remember to be your salt and light in the world. In Jesus' Name.

Amen

Psalm 100

Shout for joy to the LORD, all the earth. Worship the LORD with gladness; come before him with joyful songs. Know that the LORD is God. It is he who made us, and we are his; we are his people, the sheep of his pasture. Enter his gates with thanksgiving and his courts with praise; give thanks to him and praise his name. For the LORD is good and his love endures forever; his faithfulness continues through all generations.

MY
Prayers

_____

_____

_____

_____

_____

_____

ANSWERED
Prayers

_____

_____

_____

_____

_____

_____

_____

My Lord God,

Even amid turmoil, I understand how much your blessings uphold me. My health may fail, but your loving arms support me. I may lose everything, but your love never leaves me or forsakes me. You are my everything in this life. Thank you for sustaining me daily. In Christ's Name.

Amen

Revelation 4:7

" He said in a loud voice, "Fear God and give him glory, because the hour of his judgment has come. Worship him who made the heavens, the earth, the sea and the springs of water. "

MY
Prayers

_____
_____
_____
_____
_____
_____
_____
_____

ANSWERED
Prayers

_____
_____
_____
_____
_____
_____
_____
_____

My Lord, my God,

You made everything with life and breath. With a word, you control the winds and weather. You hold our lives in your hands. Yet, you stop and listen to our prayers and care about the details of daily lives. Thank you for allowing us to bring our needs to you in prayer. Hear us, oh Lord, and grant us your peace.

Amen

Isaiah 25:1

Lord, you are my God; I will exalt you and praise your name, for in perfect faithfulness you have done wonderful things, things planned long ago.

MY
Prayers

ANSWERED
Prayers

Oh Lord God,

Thank you for loving us despite all our faults. Thank you for reassuring us that your ways are so much better than our own. Teach us to look for your ways and trust you for the outcome. In Jesus' Name.

Amen

Acts 16:25

> About midnight Paul and Silas were praying and singing hymns to God, and the other prisoners were listening to them.

MY
Prayers

ANSWERED
Prayers

Thank you, God,

You are always good. Your decrees are just and fair. Your word is a lamp unto our feet and a guide to us. Bring us safely home at the end of our days to spend eternity with you.

Amen

Psalm 103:1

" Praise the Lord, my soul; all my inmost being, praise his holy name. "

MY
Prayers

ANSWERED
Prayers

prayers FOR REST

Our struggles and worries can become a heavy load to carry. For some, those burdens creep into our minds as we try to sleep. Instead of fighting to solve the problems ourselves, ask God to give you rest. This part looks at prayers and verses to help us rest our weary minds and bodies.

Dear Jesus,

Help me to shine your light into the darkness of the world. Also, let your light comfort me as I lay down in slumber. Guard me and protect me this night. In Jesus' Name.

Amen

Proverbs 3:24

When you lie down, you will not be afraid; when you lie down, your sleep will be sweet.

MY
Prayers

ANSWERED
Prayers

Heavenly Father,

Please hold those I love as they sleep. Bless them with your peace that surpasses understanding, give them hope that does not dim. Grow in them dreams and visions for their future and protect them with your unconditional love.

Amen

John 14:27

"Peace I leave with you; my peace I give you. I do not give to you as the world gives. Do not let your hearts be troubled and do not be afraid."

MY
Prayers

ANSWERED
Prayers

Lord,

My mind is racing as I try to sleep tonight. The stress of my life feels overwhelming right now. I can't seem to find a way through all my problems. Please, Lord, comfort me with your peace. Take my worries and grant me a peaceful night of rest. Thank you, Jesus.

Amen

Matthew 11:28

"Come to me, all you who are weary and burdened, and I will give you rest."

MY
Prayers

ANSWERED
Prayers

Lord,

Sometimes my burdens are heavy and unmanageable. Help me to remember to give all my struggles over to you. You promise me that your burdens are light. Thank you, my dearest Jesus.

Amen

Proverbs 3:24

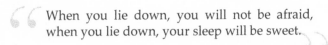

When you lie down, you will not be afraid, when you lie down, your sleep will be sweet.

MY
Prayers

ANSWERED
Prayers

My Lord,

I thank you as I watch another day come to a close. Thank you for the many blessings. Grant me peace and safety as I slumber tonight. And, if in Your will, let me awake to another new day tomorrow.

Amen

Psalm 3:5

" I lay down and slept, yet I woke up in safety, for the Lord was watching over me. "

MY
Prayers

Sovereign God,

Thank you for making our burdens light as we follow you. Thank you for showing us how to find rest for our weary souls. Please help me to remember what is most important in life. In Jesus' Name.

Amen

Psalm 116:7

" Return to your rest, my soul, for the LORD has been good to you. "

MY
Prayers

ANSWERED
Prayers

prayers
FOR STRENGTH

In the first section, we prayed for comfort from the Lord. But sometimes we need more than just support. We need God to give us the strength to conquer the battle ahead. God will provide when we go to him in prayer. This segment looks at prayers and verses to ask for God to strengthen us.

Dear Heavenly Father,

Thank you for calling us out of the pit of despair.
Help me to stay focused on the road ahead of me.
Help me not to give up and not return to my old
ways but trust fully in You. In Jesus' Name.

Amen

Isaiah 41:10

So do not fear, for I am with you; do not be dismayed, for I am your God. I will strengthen you
and help you; I will uphold you with my righteous right hand.

MY
Prayers

ANSWERED
Prayers

Dear Heavenly Father,

Thank you for the example of living a life with boldness for you. Thank you for showing us the example of praying with boldness. Please help me to follow hard after you and ignore the call of the world. In Jesus' Name.

Amen

Isaiah 40:31

"But those who hope in the Lord will renew their strength. They will soar on wings like eagles; they will run and not grow weary; they will walk and not be faint."

MY
Prayers

_____

_____

_____

_____

_____

_____

_____

ANSWERED
Prayers

_____

_____

_____

_____

_____

_____

_____

Dear Heavenly Father,

You are my rock and my strength. When troubles arise, help me to cling to you only. Calm my heart and strengthen my faith to trust in You all the days of my life. In Jesus' Name.

Amen

Psalm 73:26

> My flesh and my heart may fail, but God is the strength of my heart and my portion forever.

MY
Prayers

_____

_____

_____

_____

_____

_____

ANSWERED
Prayers

_____

_____

_____

_____

_____

_____

_____

Dear Jesus,

If our circumstances can't be changed, then strengthen us to endure every trial that comes our way.

Amen

Philippians 4:13

" I can do all this through him who gives me strength. "

MY
Prayers

ANSWERED
Prayers

Dear Jesus,

I am yours, and you are mine. Protect me from the schemes of the enemy. Protect my loved ones. Let me live my days in your safety and love. Guide me daily, my Lord. My God.

Amen

2 Timothy 1:7

For the Spirit God gave us does not make us timid, but gives us power, love and self-discipline.

MY
Prayers

ANSWERED
Prayers

Dear Lord Jesus,

Thank you for the ways you work out things for my good, even when I don't understand. When doubt fills me, please remind me of your promise in Romans 8:28. I pray for the wisdom to trust your ways. In Jesus' Name.

Amen

2 Thessalonians 3:3

" But the Lord is faithful, and he will strengthen you and protect you from the evil one. "

MY
Prayers

ANSWERED
Prayers

Dear Lord,

I seek you and your strength. I ask that your presence will always be with me. In weakness, I claim your power because You are my hiding place. I praise you. Lord, I pray for the song of deliverance so that I may receive your divine strength.

Amen

I Chronicles 16:11

"Look to the Lord and his strength; seek his face always."

MY
Prayers

ANSWERED
Prayers

Heavenly Father,

I know that you go before me, and you will not forsake me or leave me. So in my plea for strength, I will not fear or be dismayed because You are my refuge. I repent of my sins, knowing that I can rest in my salvation. Thank you, Father.

Amen

I Corinthian 6:13

"Be on your guard; stand firm in the faith; be courageous; be strong."

MY
Prayers

ANSWERED
Prayers

Heavenly Father,

Your Word declares the name of the Lord is a strong tower, and the righteous run into it. So, Lord, in the challenges of life and this battle, I declare you as my strong tower, and I run to you for safety. I stand upon your Word.

Amen

Psalm 59:16

> But I will sing of your strength, in the morning I will sing of your love; for you are my fortress, my refuge in times of trouble.

MY
Prayers

ANSWERED
Prayers

Holy Father,

Thank you for staying close to me no matter my circumstances. Please give me strength when fears surround me. Let me feel your presence and comfort me as I bring my concern to you in prayer. In Jesus' Name.

Amen

Ephesians 6:10

"Finally, be strong in the Lord and in his mighty power."

MY
Prayers

ANSWERED
Prayers

Holy Spirit,

Please encircle me, hold me safe and secure. Wrap my mind up with your truth. Guide my thoughts and calm my fears. Steady my emotions so I may not become upset by the little things. Sustain my soul. Give me your vision for the future and hope for tomorrow. I need you.

Amen

Habakkuk 3:19

The Sovereign Lord is my strength; he makes my feet like the feet of a deer, he enables me to tread on the heights.

MY
Prayers

ANSWERED
Prayers

My Heavenly Father,

Increase my faith. Change any unbelief in my heart into an unshakable faith. Strengthen your servant, so I may serve you well until you call me home. Thank you, Jesus.

Amen

Psalm 28:7

The Lord is my strength and my shield; my heart trusts in him, and he helps me. My heart leaps for joy, and with my song I praise him.

MY
Prayers

ANSWERED
Prayers

Oh God,

I thank you for who you are and for your love
and blessings over my life. Lord, because you are
in my life, I thank you for the victory over my
enemies. You are my strength and my song. You
are my God. I will forever praise you and exalt
your name.

Amen

Ephesians 3:20-21

"Now to him who is able to do immeasurably
more than all we ask or imagine, according to
his power that is at work within us, to him be
glory in the church and in Christ Jesus throughout all generations, for ever and ever! Amen."

MY
Prayers

ANSWERED
Prayers

Dearest Heavenly Father,

Please grant me your strength to share your words and gifts with others around me. Please teach me your ways and your words to use. Thank you for always standing by my side in all circumstances. In Jesus' Name, I pray.

Amen

1 Corinthians 1:18

" For the message of the cross is foolishness to those who are perishing, but to us who are being saved it is the power of God. "

MY
Prayers

ANSWERED
Prayers

SPECIAL

prayers

Across various Christian denominations, specific prayers have become known. These prayers all honor and serve the Lord as excellent worship tools and will find a place in your prayer life when you face certain situations and seasons in your life. Pray them out loud, journal them, expound on them and make them your own.

The Serenity Prayer

by Reinhold Niebuhr

God, grant me the serenity to accept the things I cannot change, the courage to change the things I can, and the wisdom to know the difference. Living one day at a time, enjoying one moment at a time; accepting hardship as a pathway to peace; Taking, as Jesus did, this sinful world as it is, not as I would have it; trusting that You will make all things right if I surrender to your will; so that I may be reasonably happy in this life and supremely happy with you forever in the next.

Amen

MY
Prayers

ANSWERED
Prayers

Child's Bedtime Prayer

Now I lay me down to sleep; I pray the Lord my soul to keep, watch, and guard me through the night and wake me with the morning light.

Amen.

MY
Prayers

ANSWERED
Prayers

The Lord's Prayer

Our Father, which art in Heaven, Hallowed be thy Name. Thy Kingdom come. Thy will be done on earth, As it is in Heaven. Give us this day our daily bread. And forgive us our trespasses, as we forgive them that trespass against us. And lead us not into temptation; But deliver us from evil. For thine is the kingdom, The power, and the glory, Forever and ever.

Amen.

MY
Prayers

ANSWERED
Prayers

Catholic Prayer

Come Holy Spirit, fill the hearts of your faithful and kindle in them the fire of your love. Send forth your Spirit, and they shall be created. And You shall renew the face of the earth. O, God, who by the light of the Holy Spirit, did instruct the hearts of the faithful, grant that by the same Holy Spirit we may be truly wise and ever enjoy His consolations, Through Christ Our Lord,

Amen.

MY
Prayers

ANSWERED
Prayers

St Patrick's

Prayer for strength

Christ with me, Christ before me, Christ behind me, Christ in me, Christ beneath me, Christ above me, Christ on my right, Christ on my left, Christ when I lie down, Christ when I sit down, Christ when I arise, Christ in the heart of every man who thinks of me, Christ in the mouth of everyone who speaks of me, Christ in every eye that sees me, Christ in every ear that hears me.

Amen.

MY
Prayers

ANSWERED
Prayers

Covenant Prayer

by John Wesley

I am no longer my own, but yours. Put me to what you will; place me with whom you will. Put me to doing, put me to suffering. Let me be put to work for you or set aside for you, praised for you, or criticized for you. Let me be full; let me be empty. Let me have all things, let me have nothing. I freely and fully surrender all things to your glory and service. And now, O wonderful and holy God, Creator, Redeemer, and Sustainer, you are mine, and I am yours. So be it. And the covenant which I have made on earth, let it also be made in Heaven.

Amen.

MY
Prayers

ANSWERED
Prayers

Instrument of Your Peace

by St. Francis of Assisi

Lord, make me an instrument of your peace. Where there is hatred, let me sow love. Where there is injury, pardon, where there is doubt, faith, where there is despair, hope, where there is darkness, light, where there is sadness, joy. O Divine Master, grant that I may not so much seek to be consoled as to console, not so much to be understood as to understand, not so much to be loved, as to love; for it is in giving that we receive, it is in pardoning that we are pardoned, it is in dying that we awake to eternal life.

Amen

MY
Prayers

ANSWERED
Prayers

Lead Us Prayer

by St. Augustine

Lead us, O God, from the sight of the lovely things of the world. To the thought of thee their Creator; and grant that delighting in the beautiful things of thy creation, we may delight in thee, the first author of beauty and the Sovereign Lord of all thy works, blessed forevermore.

Amen

MY
Prayers

ANSWERED
Prayers

Let Me Serve You Prayer

St. Theresa of Avilla

Govern everything by your wisdom, O Lord, so that my soul may always be serving you in the way you will and not as I choose. Let me die to myself so that I may serve you; let me live to you who are live itself.

Amen

MY
Prayers

ANSWERED
Prayers

praying
SCRIPTURE

One of the most effective ways to speak to God is simply reciting his Word. Open your bible and you will find many verses that will relate to your situation and make it easy to open up a dialogue of prayer. These scripture verses are a few examples. Add to these with your own favorites.

Pray Acts 4:29-30 (NLT)

"Give me, your servant, great boldness in preaching your word. Stretch out your hand with healing power; may miraculous signs and wonders be done through the name of your holy servant Jesus."

Amen.

MY
Prayers

ANSWERED
Prayers

Pray Matthew 9:37-38

"Heavenly Father, the harvest is plentiful, but the laborers are few. Lord, I pray to you to send more laborers into the harvest so all people will hear of your saving grace."

Amen

MY
Prayers

ANSWERED
Prayers

Pray Exodus 33:13 (NLT)

"If it is true that you look favorably on me, let me know your ways, so I may understand you more fully and continue to enjoy your favor."

Amen

MY
Prayers

ANSWERED
Prayers

Pray Colossians 1:9-12

"Lord, I pray I will be filled with the knowledge of your will in all spiritual wisdom and understanding to walk in a manner worthy of you Lord, fully pleasing to you, bearing fruit in every good work and increasing in the knowledge of you. I pray for you to strengthen me with all power according to your glorious might, for all endurance and patience with joy, giving thanks to the Father, who has qualified me to share in the inheritance of the saints in light."

Amen.

MY
Prayers

ANSWERED
Prayers

Pray 1 Chronicles 4:10 (NLT)

"Oh, that you would bless me and expand my territory! Please be with me in all that I do and keep me from all trouble and pain!"

Amen.

MY
Prayers

ANSWERED
Prayers

Pray Psalm 51:7, 10-12

"Purify me from my sins, and I will be clean wash me, and I will be whiter than snow. Create in me a clean heart, O God, renew a loyal spirit within me. Do not banish me from your presence, and don't take your Holy Spirit from me. Restore to me the joy of your salvation and make me willing to obey you."

Amen.

MY
Prayers

ANSWERED
Prayers

Pray the 23rd Psalm

"The Lord is my shepherd; I shall not want. He makes me lie down in green pastures: he leadeth me beside the still waters. He restoreth my soul: he leadeth me in the paths of righteousness for his Name's sake. Yea, though I walk through the valley of the shadow of death, I will fear no evil: for thou art with me; thy rod and thy staff they comfort me. You prepare a table before me in the presence of mine enemies: thou anointed my head with oil; my cup runs over. Surely goodness and mercy shall follow me all the days of my life: and I will dwell in the house of the Lord forever."

Amen.

MY
Prayers

ANSWERED
Prayers

Pray Luke 18:13 (ESV)

"God, be merciful to me, a sinner."

Amen.

MY
Prayers

ANSWERED
Prayers

Pray Psalm 25:1-2, 4-6

" In You, Lord my God, I put my trust. I trust in you;
do not let me be put to shame, nor let my enemies'
triumph over me. Show me your ways, Lord, teach
me your paths. Guide me in yYour truth and teach
me, for you are God my Savior, and my hope is in
you all day long. "

Amen.

MY
Prayers

ANSWERED
Prayers

Pray Numbers 6:24-26

"May the Lord bless me and protect me. May the Lord smile on me and be gracious to me. May the Lord show me his favor and give me his peace."

Amen.

MY
Prayers

ANSWERED
Prayers

Pray Philippians 4:7

"May the peace of God, which transcends all understanding, guard my heart and mind in Christ Jesus."

Amen

MY
Prayers

_____

_____

_____

_____

_____

_____

ANSWERED
Prayers

_____

_____

_____

_____

_____

_____

Pray 2 Corinthians 13:14

"May the grace of our Lord Jesus Christ, and the love of God, and the fellowship of the Holy Spirit be with us all, now and evermore."

Amen

MY
Prayers

ANSWERED
Prayers

Pray Philippians 1:9-11

"Dear Father. I pray this for my family and friend. May your love may abound even more and more in knowledge and every kind of insight so that you can decide what is best, and thus be sincere and blameless for the day of Christ, filled with the fruit of righteousness that comes."

Amen

MY
Prayers

ANSWERED
Prayers

YVONNE M. MORGAN

Yvonne M. Morgan is a wife, mother, and grandmother passionate about missions and sharing the amazing stories of Christ in action witnessed by believers placing their trust in Him. She hopes that her writing and mission work inspires others to seek God in the turmoil of life, and to be the hands and feet of Jesus to others in their struggles.

As the founder of the Orphan Relief Effort, she has led the charity for nearly 20 years, to support orphanages in Nepal and Myanmar and provides care for 50 children.

Outside of her work in missions, Yvonne is a full-time writer. She is the author of, Turning Mountains into Molehills, a memoir of her personal journey in the mission field. She also posts to a blog with the same name. Her first children's book, Sad Little Wildflower, will be released in the fall of 2020.

Yvonne was born in Belfast, Northern Ireland, and lived in Canada before moving to the US with her family in 1973. Since then she has developed a deep passion for traveling and mission work. Her travels have taken her to 42 countries on five continents, 49 US states (still hoping to visit Alaska), and eight provinces in Canada. When not writing, traveling, or working in the mission field, she enjoys her family and four wonderful granddaughters. She lives in Edmond, Oklahoma with her husband, Bill.

CPSIA information can be obtained
at www.ICGtesting.com
Printed in the USA
JSHW030724061020
8454JS00004B/10

9 780997 912685